The Builder

by **Kari James**

illustrated by **Manuel King**

Scott Foresman

Editorial Offices: Glenview, Illinois • New York, New York
Sales Offices: Reading, Massachusetts • Duluth, Georgia
Glenview, Illinois • Carrollton, Texas • Menlo Park, California

I build buildings.
I build buildings in the city.
I build buildings in the country.

People live in some of
my buildings.
People work in some of
my buildings.

Today I am building a new house . . . with just one room!
Here are the plans.
The plans are like a map. They show how the house will look.

Yesterday I dug a hole.
Now I am filling it up.

I wait for it to dry.
Then I am ready to build.

I cover it with wood.

Then I put down the floor.
It is made of wood too.

Up go the high walls!
On goes the roof!

Now it is time to put in the door and windows.
This place is starting to look good!

Now I am sealing the
roof to keep the house dry.

Now I am covering the walls.
Doesn't this place look good?

Now I dig some holes.
And I plant some trees.

I like to build buildings . . .

for my friends!